Inappropriate Behaviour

Inappropriate Behaviour by Tim Lander 2006.

Front cover photo by Tim Lander.
Back cover potrait of the poet by R.W. Sinclair.
Design and in-house editing by the publisher, Joe Blades.
Printed and bound in Canada by Sentinel Printing, Yarmouth NS.
Broken Jaw Press is an affiliate of Access Copyright: www.accesscopyright.ca

Acknowledgements
   Most of these poems were previously published in chapbooks, and while the
poet reserves his moral rights of authorship, they are declared "copy free" under
the terms of the Copyright Act. An earlier version of "The Ballad of Ronny
Walker" under the title "Ronny Walker" was first published in *Street Heart Poems*
(Nanaimo: private, 1993), a hand-written, photocopied book published by the
poet; later hand-set, printed and published as a chapbook by Rusty North (Port
Townsend, WA: Sagitarrius Press, 1999. "The Gods" was published in *Vancouver
Poems*, ed Allan Safarik (Vancouver, Polestar Books, 1986), and in *Street Heart
Poems* (Nanaimo: private, 1993). "How They Made a Man of Me" was published
in *Prism International*, 2002. "Mea Cupa" in *Street Heart Poems* (Nanaimo: private,
1993). "Pecunia Non Olet" published by Ed Varney (Vancouver/Montreal: The
Poem Factory/Usine de poeme, 1995).
   Do not reproduce without love.
   The author may be reached at: Tim Lander, Box 996, Nanaimo BC V9R 5N2,
Canada. Email: Lander_Tim@yahoo.com

The poet acknowledges the support of the Canada Council for the Arts in the
preparation of chapbook material for trade publication.

The publisher acknowledges the support of the Canada Council for the Arts and the
New Brunswick Department of Wellness, Culture and Sport.

Broken Jaw Press Inc.
Box 596 Stn A   www.brokenjaw.com
Fredericton NB E3B 5A6
Canada

Cataloguing in Publication Data

Lander, Tim
 Inappropriate behaviour / Tim Lander.

Poems.
Includes bibliograhical references.
ISBN-13: 978-1-55391-038-1
ISBN-10: 1-55391-038-9

 I. Title.

PS8573.A535I53 2006   C811'.54   C2006-904243-8

Inappropriate Behaviour

Tim Lander

Fredericton • Canada

La poesia se ha portado bien
Yo me portado horriblemente mal
Nicanor Parra

INAPPROPRIATE BEHAVIOUR

Preface

Sitting in Rusty's kitchen showing her a proof copy of this book and reading a chapbook which was on her table, poems by a friend of hers, well ritten and competently typeset on a computer, I asked Rusty if she found my work legible. She said yes, though she had problems with a few words. I said I tryed to make my work untidy but legible then went back to the book I was reading, but still my mind was on the implications of what I had just said. In the book there were strong lines, weak lines, impassioned lines, relaxed lines, funny lines, ironic lines, tender lines sad lines, bitter lines, all in the same mechanical typeface that marched across the page like a train jogging through a landscape. One line I came to I thought "I'd love to see this line in handwriting." for me handwriting is like live reading—see the hand of the poet, hear the voice of the poet. I try to read with clarity (sometimes in my toothless condition this must be struggled for) but with passion remembering Blake's admonition: "to be in a passion you good may do, but no good if a passion is in you" like—don't overload unless you like swimming with the sharks, passion is energy—but you don't want no chain reaction, or perhaps you do.

In this book I have stept beyond the bounds of spelling and kerect grammar. In the old days, when you were a child, first you learnt to form letters, in beautiful copperplate, then you learnt to spell the words and when those two enormous taskes were accomplished, you learnt to use those words to express yourself, but ironically you had been expressing yourself very adequately all along, in the schoolyard and within your family, so learning to write was not so much learning to express, but learning to record expression.

When I was at school we were always told "If you don't know how to spell, you don't know how to write". I never made a success of spelling, and English spelling for me is still full of bitter memories, and psychological conflicts, it was like a wild dog to me, of which I was afraid and which knew my fear. I was punished for my spelling and grew up thinking I couldn't write, because I was a timid child who believed his teachers.

We were also told not to talk, let alone write using "Bad Grammar" the language of the "lower classes" or we would sound like "Yobs" or "Guttersnipes". Much later I discovered that the "Lower Classes" spoke a debased remnant of Anglo-Saxon, while the middle classes strove to imitate the Anglo-Norman of the aristocracy "after the scole of Stratford atte bowe" (Chaucer's Prioress was a cockney, and her dad was a teamster who of course swore by St Loy), and later they adopted the neo-classicism of the Age of 'Enlightenment'.

I started to find it fun, indeed liberating to write in the language of my preschool childhood, how I shouldn't ought to have writ, a bit like throwing snowballs at the Headmaster.

The first aesthetic principle for the creative artist is "If it is fun, do it!" and that is a good slogan to throw in the teeth of the uprising puritans.

Though I am in love with the photocopier I admit to being a philosophical Luddite. We have succumbed too easily to domination by the machine. Rage against the Machine. Rage against the dying of the Light.

I w'd like to write poetry that computers can't read, that spell checks balk at and grammar checks reject, that is not 'Standard English' for no one's language is 'standard' It just ain't the way we speak.

Tim Lander
Trying to Ryt a Poim (2000)

MISTER POIT

I am a poit
 they say
"Mister Poit, Mister Poit
 look into the future
tell us wot u see"

so I look and C
and tell them wot I C

 then they say
"We don't want to hear
 none of that
  that's not wot we call poetry
Tell us wot we want to hear"

"I no wot U want to hear" I say
"Well unlimited sex
 but there's nothing wrong
  with that

let's get down and dirty
 in the garden of delite
and spin some floral metaphors—

A rose is a briar
 is a pasture for aphids
and aphids love roses
 as much as lovers do
when the sweet juice of the rose bud
 is ripe for their sucking

and in the garden of love
 grows good weed—hey man
let's rub our flesh together
 plug in our nervous systems"

All the old words
 have been said so well already
"My love is like the daffadowndilly
 fair as the rose, soft as the lily"

but wot we got
 is small change to play with
the window of the future
 the steamed up window
to write, like children
 our love-notes on
to draw our crossed hearts on—

"Old Poit, Ol' Poit
 tel me wot U no of it"

the dance we dance on
 back into history and off to the future
 got sum dreaming to do
  the old soft shoo

and off you spin us
 like a spider
down the murky passages
 of time to come

Cum dance with me
 in history
at the beginning and end
 of history

Cum dance with me
 at the cockroach ball
 at the roach hotel
  in Vegas
with its Picassos
 Renoirs and Pollocks
Dekoonings and Degas

not to mention Van G
elevated to that whorehouse in the sky
 the million dollar roach hotel
  by Lake Como
  in Vegas

Come dance with me
 li'l magot
  chew on the flesh
   of the super rich
    in Vegas

U sa Ol' Poit, Ol' Poit
 sing us a song
so I climd on the stove
 and sang them a song

"the futur's ful of wunderment
 old newspapers
  and cockroach wings
but nothin like U think

Hey U with the RRSP
 wot U think U gonna se
don't cum and ask no advis off me
 ther's sum wot's bound
and sum wot's free
 cum dance with me
round that ol apple tree

ther's one thing that we all agree
 the rivers all flow down to the sea
  there's a snake in that there apple tree
   and it's cockroaches, it's cockroaches
we'll all be reborn as cockroaches

 and so . . .

Published in *Trying to Ryt a Poim*, 2000.

MEA CULPA

Yes
　I admit the fact
　I'm a street poet
　　panhandling old poems
round the streets of Vancouver

"Do you want to buy a poem
　for a penny?
　Poems penny each!
W'd you care for a poem, sir?
　Only a penny
　　Nothing round here
　you can get any cheaper
but of course
　if you give me
　　a dime or a quarter
　I won't say "No"
　　even to a loonie
Take a few poems
　yeah, help yourself
I'm learning how to bake them
　into cookies"

Sewing books together
　on the ferry from Nanaimo
I take them round the English profs
　at UBC
　　browbeat them
into buying
　slender hand written books
run off on a photocopier

But it's poetry
　Oh yes, they like the drawings
but it's poetry
　as good, no better
　than any other

Maybe I lack the skill and subtlety
　of language poets

or deconstructionalists
 or destructivists
or post modern post historical
 post literate post coital
  post partum post mortem
   poets

 But I'll sell you poetry
it's bonafide poetry
I'm a plain poet
 with a romantic touch
  of rhetoric

   and weak verbs
I admit I have weak verbs
 but I got trained
  with the best of 'em
and you can understand
 wot I say

So I'm an alien
 an expatriot
  a product—well
I was born when Hitler
 was marching into Austria
and was one year old
 when he took a crack at Poland

 so we got out of London
 headed for the Northland
  living out of suitcases
   in Wordsworth Country
   Swallows and Amazons Country
   Beatrix Potter Country
while our Dad went off
 got made into a sailor

then they sent us a telegram
 to say that he'd gone missing
"Very sorry, Madam, but we somehow
 lost your husband"
gone to that dreamland

of lost toys, old shoes
  and favorite pieces of string

Well, a very typical
  warfractured childhood
sent off to boarding school
  at six years old
learnt how to masturbate
  when I was fourteen
learnt calculus and Latin
  and all the properties
of the compounds of Calcium
  and fell out the bottom
of the old boy system

called up by her Majesty
  to her British Royal Army
to watch the red sun setting
  on her Imperial empire
at 18 in Malaya
  digging up bombs
  left behind
by the Imperial Japanese
under a tropic sun
  all for the fun of it
  at mid-day too

falling in love
  off the back of a truck
  no words
but Aug und Augenwiede
  at a distance
off the back of a truck

  and returned
to grey foggy London
  redbrick university
with the mummified corps
  of our founder
  Jeremy Bentham
  in the front hall
"The greatest good

to the greatest number"
 of maggots

So became acquainted
 with Geology, the Quantum theory
 the finer points of evolution
 and the female anatomy

   well
the army had damaged
 my leaning facility
  and my moral fibre
fell by the wayside
 became a "ban the bomber"
fell for a girl
 from the Beatles other city
briefly saw the inside
 of HM Prison
Birmingham Jail man
 but not the one
  of that old blues song

got her pregnant
 and became a husband
somehow lost the baby
 twix the cup and the lip

then failed disgracefully
 to become a teacher
 of unteachably alive
  Black Country kids

they wouldn't swallow math
 from my toffee nose accent
"I say you chaps
 let's have a bit of quiet"

well not quite that bad
 but I never was the type
  to regiment the soul
 and always known myself
  for marching out of step

and not even to that
Different Drummer

then settled for being
 a lab tech at London Zoo
husbandman to the Queen's own mice
 while my better half was busy
  planning nuclear reactors

 then, later
sitting under the Canadian Rockies
 in a London laundromat
  the day Kennedy was shot
decided to be a Canadian
 and a street poet

well, I mean
 those mountains looked
  so damned much like
   freedom and happiness
and that poor marriage
 was already written
  in something like
   a past tense

Well I have indeed
 done some useful things
  since I set my feet
   upon these shores

I've helped:
 carpenters
 bakers
  librarians
   printers
the hostler at the CPR
 rubbin' down the diesels
  giving 'em a nose bag
of oats of a frosty night
 a tank full of fuel
 a hopper full of sand

and driven
 school busses
  taxis
   hospital busses
planted trees
 dug clams
taught mathematics
 for her Majestie's prisoners
  at her Majestie's local jail

Oh I've done all sorts
 of honest to goodness things
studied sewage treatment
 water treatment
  drama
middle english literature
 Chinese history
oriental philosophy
 entomology
  invertebrate psychology

a smattering of German, French
 a smaller smattering of Spanish
  a passing acquaintance
   with a few hundred disreputable
    Chinese characters
a fumbling of John Dowland
   (Semper Dolens)
  on the guitar

all these things
 and many others like them
  make up the goulash
   of my poetry

but as I say
 I don't do 'creative writing'
  I try to make poetry
"But What"
 to quote the pepsi commercial
  "'s the diff?"
"It's in the taste" the angel says

I've a daughter who's a CA
  another a tattoo artist
a son who's a bike courier
  round the streets of Vancouver
    another who's an engineering student
and a third who's exulting
  in teenage sexuality

I'm 54 years old
  tho I've a card to say I'm 55
so I get a free cup of tea
  at Wendy's restaurant
    if I buy myself
    a hamburger

I've been married twice
  at three years a time
    and once lived common-law
      for 20 long years

and now I'm in love
  with at least one other woman
    living on the far borders
    of my consciousness
somewhere down the inevitable hiway
  on the wind naked coast

Mea culpa, Mea fuckin' culpa!

and my favorite poet
  Long Will of Ludgate Hill
Jeff Chaucer's hippy friend
  who wrote of Piers Plowman
    and the 7 deadly sins
    Mea fuckin' Culpa

William Langland or Langley
a long thin man in a threadbare gown
  spent his life improving
    his one long poem
    of Heaven and hell
and everything between

and I too have been
 on Malvern Hills
inducted in the army
 in that cold October
  of Suez and Hungary
   screaming headlines
of the dying thrusts
 of imperialism

at #1 Training Regiment
 Royal Engineers
  under the shadow
   of Malvern Hills

and hammered trilobites
 from the Langley Shales
  outcropping in a stream bed
   where cattle came to water

and walked up Ludgate Hill
 along Fleet Street where
  Dr Johnson flourished

and I too
  have sat
  with Bertrand Russell
   at the Cenotaph
    in the cold November rain

You think I am not worthy
 OK so I'm not worthy
Mea Culpa, Mea Fuckin' Culpa

and stolen a woman
 from a professorial
  Gov Gen award winning
   poet

She was the kind of girl
 who should have married
  her professor

but he was already married
  to a Great Canadian Novelist

and she never forgave me
  for not being
  a better poet
and I her subequal

  Well

and today the idea
  that excites me most
  is the concept of Gaia

the concept that the natural order
  is not one of competition
but one of balance and harmony

and the idea
  that the boundaries
  between different colonies
    of living cells
are somewhat permeable
  and to a large extent illusiary

and that our place
  on this planet
  is somewhat different
from what we've always imagined it
  to be

that the concept of Gaia
  is a strong
  biopoetic idea

a more imaginative
  and subtle way
  of looking at
    established facts

than the old
  capitalistic notion

"of survival of the fittest"

the cannibalistic notion
of
 "let the weak go under"

Indeed
 it is the unified field theory
  of the sciences of life
   love
    God
     and Poetry

and maybe viruses
 are Mother's little helpers

and then that other idea
 that history
  and herstory
   are one vast tragedy
  drawing to its final scene
and that we are about
to be overwhelmed
 in our complaisancy
  by an avalanche
   of insoluable problems

so the stage will soon be littered
 with corpses
like a Jacobean tragedy

that we shall almost live to see
 the finality
  of history

Written in response to a request for a Curriculum Vitae
from the Poetry Marketing Board of Canada. 1992.
Published in *Street Heart Poems*, 1993.

HOW THEY MADE A MAN OF ME
The initiation of a National Service Man

And in those days
 they said they'd make a man of me

They gave me a scratchy battle dress
 and a pair of boots to shine
told me to climb on the pot bellied stove
 and sing
  well yes I sang to them!

Made me yell and charge across a muddy field
 in my shiny boots
and thrust a bayonet deep in the mortal guts
 of a bag of straw
and I yelled and thrust
 and thrust again and yelled

Gave me a pick-axe handle
 and told me to stand guard
  long winter nights
that Christmas when the I.R.A.
 looted an armory
  just down the road
so we marched around in the night
 swinging our axe handles
  smoking in doorways
getting our Christmas nip
 from the sergeants' wives

And in those days
 it was all Suez and Hungary
  and the Commies
   knocking loudly on the door
nor were the Egyptians
 acting much like gentlemen
while we learnt our drill
 backwards and forwards
  up and down the old parade ground
  every day

"Slope Arms! Present Arms! Order Arms!
About Turn! At the Double Mark Time!"

They said they'd make a man of me

They gave me an old gun
 told me how I'd learn to love it
 like it was my favorite girl
Showed me how to point it at a person
 two hundred yards away
 hold my breath
 and gently squeeze—not blinking
then it jumped into my shoulder
 showed me how to work the bolt
 shove another bullet
 up the hole
and squeeze again
 all in five seconds
 (or was it three?
 I do forget)
the accurate dispensation of death
 and I learnt it all unthinking
learnt their lesson
 how to be a man
and the accurate dispensation of death

And what were women for
 we learnt that too unthinking
and how to use them
 we learnt that on the side
 from the old soldiers
 with their brothel talk

"Such a piece of equipment
 and this is what you call the parts
and this is what you use them for
 Any questions?
And keep your equipment clean"

Doing it all by numbers
 "One two three
 One two three

One"
"About Turn
  at the double Dismiss!"

"Squad will advance, by the right, quick march
  Squad will retreat, about turn
    double march"

They taught me how to be a man

"Polish y'r boots
  Blanco y'r gaiters
    Shine y'r buckles til you can see y'r face in 'em"
Little circles
  little circles
    a hot spoon to smooth away
      the pimples in y'r boot leather

"Bags of Bull"
  they said
    "Bags of Bull"
"It's not bullshit. It's Personal Pride"
  they said
    "There's no Bullshit in the British Army"*

Kit all folded to the size of a mess tin
  mess tin polished til you can see y'r ugly mug in it
    you don't never put no food in it
      you'd spoil the shine
you got another
  old greasy one
    you keep well out of sight
that's wot you take
  when you go down to the cookhouse

"Polish y'r boots
  drink y'r beer
    fall in for church parade
Sing hymns to God
  and his British Empire"

I am a man
'cos that's wot they made of me
gave me a number
to remember all my life

"two, double three, double four,
five six two
Sapper Lander, Sir"

"Wot do you think this is?
a fucking garden party?
Wot's y'r name and number, sapper?"
"23344562, SAPPER LANDER. SIR!"
"That's better.
Say it like you're proud of it.
I don't want any one in my troop
Who's not proud to be a Sapper.
Right?"
"Right. Sir!"

"Get y'r feet down hard!"
"You horrible little man. What are you?
"A horrible little man, sir"
"WOT R U?"
"A HORRIBLE LITTLE MAN. SIR."
"Why can't you keep in step
you horrible little man?
You march like a pregnant duck
You look like a bag of shit
tied together
with a string round the middle"

So they made a man of me

"Come on, let's have you!"
"Hands off your cocks and on with your socks!"
"Get y'r feet on the floor!"
Make y'r bed, lay out y'r kit
fall in on the road
march down to breakfast

"Stand by y'r beds!"
"Wot's this? You call this a straight line?
  Get out y'r piece of string
  line it all up again"
The beds, socks, underwear
 spare cap badge
"There's dust here sapper
 y'r on a charge
Report to the guardroom after parade"

Out on the parade ground
 up and down
or "today we're going to build us a bridge,
 you lucky lads"
Twelve men to a bridge panel
 "All together. Lift. Quick March"

night exercises
 stumbling in the dark
  same old bridge
  same old mud hole

Church parade
 Pray for the sergeant's soul
  Down to the sick bay
   Roll up y'r sleeves
    jab it in
"No drinking for 48 hours
 or you'll be right back in
  for another shot."

then with sore arms
 and inflamed lymph nodes
  sent home on leave
in scratchy uniforms
 back to our mums
  for a long weekend
   to dance with the girls
"It's not that bad really
 I can take it"
to their soft
 unmilitary eyes

and all to make sure
  it was
that the sun
on the British Empire
  set
in an orderly fashion.

(I wunder wot I'd av dun
if the army ad been
  the Wehrmacht
and the year '39.

*This is quoted from an answer given in the House of Commons when
a Nation Service Man's mother complained through her MP about
her son wasting his time and the taxpayers' money on unnecessary
polishing, etc.

1998. Published in *Trying to Ryt a Poim*, 2000.

A DAY IN THE LIFE OF A STREET POET

The sound of traffic
  on the street above
   the sun filtering through
   the new leafed bushes
Turn a few times to continue dreaming
 listen to the twitter of little birds
   the squark of geese
and the bark and whistle of early morning dog walkers
the drum of traffic on the hiway far above

Decide by the height of the sun
  time to get moving
   get a move on
   get a life
my shirt bundled by my head
 30 bucks in change
  from the previous evening
all the stuff from my pockets
 stashed in my sleeping bag

Pick my dentures out of my hat
 shove them in my mouth
  to feel a lump inside them
pull them out again
 to find a little black beetle
  walking through the canyon where my gums go
knock him off, send him scurrying
 through the grass—better place for a beetle
  than in my mouth—the miasma of my breath

So glasses to nose, socks to feet
 pull on my well ventilated summer shoes
  bought in Port Angeles
  to keep out the New Years snow

Hat to head, take a pee
 shoulder my pack
  pick up my shopping bag
push my way through the bushes
 down the slope to where the yuppies jog

padding past in their well cared for yuppie bodies
Who cares what they think of an old man
 with a long beard emerging like some
ancient god come down for a walkabout?

Up past the brewery onto Burrard Street
 to join the world of traffic
  and the sweet smell of fermentation
up to 3rd Ave and over a block
 through the hard edged geometry
  to Mr B's Convenience Store
   Breakfast, a photocopier and hospitality
Set down my backpack
 find I've left my haversack
  back at my sleeping spot.

I throw my backpack behind the garbage can
 and say:
  "Is it OK if I leave it there?
I'll be back in a minute,
 left something behind"
  He nods permission

Back down behind the Brewers
 and the Seaforth Highland parking lot
to the old railroad tracks
 bulk cars of barley
  all that keeps them alive
   relics of a more industrial age—
Memories of walking the trestle across False Creek
 from Claire's little cabin on Clay's Wharf
  30 years ago

So back to my sleeping spot
 to find my bag there waiting
  my notebooks within it
Walk back to Mr B's for Earl Grey tea
 and a cinnamon roll, a sinnerman myself
  give him all my 30 bucks
   in change for notes, he asks:
"Where do you get it all from?"
 "Selling poems round the streets"

I'm not very forthcoming,
  kind of secretive about my affairs
  but he's glad of the change.

When I've eaten my bun
  I ask him to turn on his photocopier
   make five copies of each sheet of poems,
    pay for my copies
take them back to my table
  get some more water for my tea bag
  and look for a piece of cardboard
so I don't cut up his table.

I get out my utility knife
  click out the blade
   and cut between the poems
till I have a nice pile of bits of paper—
  Well five sheets—I make five piles
   dealing them from the top of the stack
   so the poems don't pad together
five piles each with all the poems
  collated on the table

I put them in my hat
  then pull on my work hat
   (a red and blue magician's hat
    with a tassel on the top,
     which cost me 10 bucks at
      Little Tibet in Victoria.
A silver sun sewn on the front,
  a big yellow Delai Lama
   button on the side and a snake at the back
    it all adds 3 inches to my height
though I hardly need them)

Shoulder my pack,
  pick up my bags
   say "Good Day" to Mr B
and head off to Granville Island
 Across the causeway,
  underneath the main span
  of Granville Bridge

which dominates the island,
 far above the roofs.

On one side of the causeway
 a marina where Clay's Wharf used to be
  Back in '64 Claire Weintraub lived there
come from New York to join the creative writing class
 at UBC.
  We used to sit together with a bunch of cronies
at the back of the theatre history class
 and argue with Dr Strassmann,
  gave him a hard time

Well I painted the little cottage on the wharf for her
 twelve foot ceilings, smoke marked from the wood stove,
  but a month after we had finished
   Old Man Clay gave her her notice
   he said that she was dirty
well I guess we got the job done for him
 Her with her limp like Rosa Luxemberg
  and her snow white Samoyed called Sanchi

And I a naive Englishman
 who didn't know which end was up
  and still I don't

We met at a poetry reading
 at Simon's Ear Coffee house
  a poet droning on and on
she fell asleep beside me
 a cautionary tale for the boring
  would be practitioners
   of the art of poetry
you'll have your audience
 sleeping together and snoring

Claire, If you read these lines
 where ever you are I salute you.

But now where her house was
 it's all plastic yachts,

paddle boats, Adrenalin Sports
and racks of toy kayaks

and where the sawmill used to be
 is condominiums, landscaped
  waterscaped with a duck pond
in a huge one acre plastic sheet
 or something like that
  you can see the plastic sticking up
   above the dirt around the edges
virtual reality—

So I walk across the causeway
 with its old embedded archeologic
  railroad tracks to the island
that mudbank in False Creek
 given over to half a century of industry
  now breathed to life again with
public market, craft stores, artist studios
 and Vancouver's art college
  misnamed for a woman from Victoria
  who went out and painted
the great trees of the forest
and became BC's token artist
 Klee Wyk the smiling one

Well how does that fit in?
 She, a free spirit slightly dotty
  ran a boarding house and now
has an enormous institution, a
 Kulture factory named after her
  building another wing too
   for 50 million dollars,
    govt support for the arts
but it's all back to front and they
 certainly don't know which end is up

So I walk along
 in my sleepy private space
Gotta get public as I walk on the Island
 past the sailmakers and the printmakers

and a guy crosses the road to me
  and says:
"Hey, you're the poet!"
  Can I have a couple of poems?
So I get them out of my pocket
 in their plastic bag, and say
  "I hope you like them"
he gives me a quarter

The day has started
 though my head is not in gear
  I feel an inherent resistance
   in my spirit
to all those confrontations

Not many people about
 and those that are there
  are all walking with a purpose—

Not much happening
 at this time of morning
  so I swing my pack off my shoulder
   just by the market entrance
Get out my piccolo
 put the case on the ground
  throw a few coins in it
"Salting the hat" they call it

Sound a few tentative notes
 adjusting my embouchure
  trills and scales
   and tonguings and fingerings
start accosting the passers by
 "Poems Penny Each"
  "No thanks"
"Wanna buy a poem for a penny?"
 "Not today, thanks"
"Pick a poem, I'll read it ya"
 "Lovely day for a poem"
  "What else can you buy for a Penny?"

And a hundred times they say:
 "NO" or "Nope" or "That's OK"
"I write my own"
 "Got lots at home"
 "Got too much to read anyway"
"I work for my money"
"What do you think I'm doing?" I ask
 I'm becoming a collector of "No"s

Sometimes I feel like I'm talking
 across a great divide
"A Poem" I say "A Poem for a Penny!"
 It amazes me the people who say "No"
  coming out of the art galleries
  and pottery studios
No they don't want their lives
 invaded by my poetry
not even for a penny
 though I can hardly blame them
Poetry is never what y'd expect it to be—

And then the strangest
 most unlikely people say "Yes"
"Surely it's worth more than a penny"
 "Will you read it to me?"
  "Do I get to keep it?"

Or kids come
 "can I have a poem?"
So I look for one
 of my little animal poems
"Dog poems, Cat poems
 Ant poems, Cockroach poems
Nice poems, Nasty poems
 Kids poems, Adult poems"

But with all those "No"s I get
 sometimes it's easier
  to get out my flute
just stand there and play it
 it makes a nice noise
  though I'm no musician

Just play a bunch of scales
 and trills, tonguings and fingerings
and if the people say they like it
 I say "I'm just practicing, I'm
really selling poems. I'm just learning
 how to play it, though I admit
I'm getting better.
     W'd you like to take a poem?"

Then I shoulder my pack
 and walk around the people
  sitting on the wharf
eating Chinese food and pizza
 off styrofoam trays
"Pick a poem and I'll read it ya"
 "W'd you like a poem today?
  Poems for every taste
and every occasion
 fully guaranteed
  worth every penny
Take one and pay me when y'r rich"

So, well,
 I do that for a little while
Stop and have a cup of tea
 and when I come back
  the guy with the pan pipes
   is setting up his PA
    just where I was standing
so I walk to the cement plant
 the heavy industrial presence
  on Granville Island—
But it's Sunday
 the gates are locked
  the trucks
   are washed out and sleeping
and the pile driver
 is not thumping
  across the road
   where they are adding
    to the art college
the great institution of culture

where poets are certainly
not welcome

Then this scene happened
  I wrote it just the way it happened
    in McDonnell's the same evening
  to perform at the poetry festival
    that happened the next day
    and that's why I said "yesterday":

"This isn't the poem I was going to perform
  I don't know if y'd call it even a poem
    maybe just
      a run of the mill complaint

Well anyway
  Yesterday I was on Granville Island
    playing my flute
      selling poems
        generally bothering the passers by
  trying to turn an honest buck
    so I can send my kid to college
      "Poems Penny Each"
      "Wanna buy a poem for a penny?"
      "Pick a poem and I'll read it ya"
  Sleeping bag draped over
    the Cement Co chain-link
      to catch the sun—get the picture?

So along comes a Granville Island cop
  didn't trouble me, I'm registered with the office
    been through all that before
  I see him coming across the road
  but see by the way he walks
    there's trouble in the wind
  I keep on playing my flute.

He says "What are you doing?"
  "Selling poems, reading them to people"
"Well we got a complaint
  from the city police

you've got to stop what y'r doing
and get off the Island!"

"Why?'

"Y'r panhandling
and the city police
 say you've got to go
  they've received complaints
   on the telephone"

"No. I'm not panhandling
I'm performing my poetry
 I'm registered at the office
  been through all this before"

"Show me you permission
Prove to me you've got it"

"Well, it's at home in Nanaimo
and it's not a signed permission
 just a set of rules they gived me"

"The office is closed because it's a holiday
and I won't believe you've got permission
 till I see it.
The City Police got complaints
 about you panhandling
  and you've got to go.
You leave the Island right now
 or do you want to talk
  to the Vancouver Police?"

He said that like a threat
 I was too shocked to be rude, or funny
  so I said to him, slow and rather tiredly
"Yes.
 I want to talk
  to the Vancouver Police
   This is my livelyhood"

He talks into his cellular
 but the cop in question
  is out somewhere eating lunch—

Then along comes Matt
 He gets all kinds of TV roles
  and once played Shakespear in Nanaimo
He's got clown makeup all over his face
 I tell him the problem
  that somehow poets
   don't make the grade
    like penny-ante musicians

He don't understand
 my cryptic narration
  but he says to the cop
"I know this man
 He's a good guy, etc
  Known him for years"
and he says to me
 "Good subject for a poem"

Well Matt goes off
 and the cop gets respectful
  as Matt is a wage earner
   and this is the poem i wrote him.
I tell the cop I'll wait for the city boys
 in the Net Loft coffee shop.

I go off to the market to buy a bag of buns
 and get a cup of tea from Suzy Q's
Sit down to listen to three lovely women
 playing classical trios on Flute Violin and Cello
for three minutes the music floods my soul
 I'm in another country

but along comes that cop again
 can't find the city guy
takes me up to the office
 by the back door entrance
which somehow now is open

The lady there is pleasant
 she remembers me
but can't remember how she remembers me
 but tells me it is not permitted
  to say: "Poems Penny Each"
  James Joyce rest in peace
"Can't give a price" she says
 and shows me the regulations
  which she highlights in yellow
and she writes me a sign that says
 "By Contribution" and she writes after
  "Thank you"

Well that upset my day a bit
 but it got me thinking
  it was not for panhandling
the cops were trying to chase me
 they mentioned telephone complaints
  anonymous denunciations
perhaps my celebrations of the erotic
 had fallen into the wrong hands
  and I don't mean kids' hands
I've already written a bunch
 of little beastie poems just for them
I'm conscientious and careful and I'm a parent
 but I'd offended perhaps some book burner
  politically incorrect
   for some four square gospel
So help me God!

And I used to think
 I'd die at age of ninety in my bed
but now I'm beginning to wonder
 if I won't be toasted
  surrounded by a pile of my own books
   as I watch our culture ripped asunder
fragmented into isolated noncommunicating
 shards of history.

What can I do but despair
 ours is the culture
  of the anonymous complaint

the anonymous denunciation
  the TIPP line
    small town bounty hunters, witness a crime
    and suddenly you might be Rich!

Salmon Rushdie y'r in good company
  the message is out
    they've got us on the run
      Bad guys don't deserve no friends!

It's all part of some iceberg or other
  watching the tides of history flow agin us
And in Victoria I've heard
  they are going to license buskers
    at 200 bucks a shot, picked out of a hat
and ban panhandlers
  least the good people
    at the Commonwealth Games might notice
      that good old home town poverty
is alive and well
  on the streets of N Amerikay as well

So the poets of Victoria
  the scruffy ones
    not the ones in *The Malahat Review*
have thought up a festival
  of scurrilous street poetry
by fax and by placard
  and by unlawful assembly
    lest sport be nothing
      but fascist intimidation
        and that is the top
of some bloody iceberg
  and as I say Poets
are iceberg observers

And this guy comes out
  of Granville Island market
    wearing an Aryan Nations T-shirt
      so I say to him
"W'd you like a poem today, Sir?"
  but he don't say nothing

he don't look at me
"You look like you need one" I add
I thought later perhaps I sh'd have said
  "Why don't you go back to your area?"
  or maybe "pretty T-shirt"
but if you tell some poor deluded guy
 suffering from an identity crisis
  in a large way—he's an arse hole
he'll feel quite justified
 in acting like an arse hole
and we all have arse hole in us
 and are the Aryan Nations
  very much different
from yuppies who will call the cops on you
 for the offending of their dignity?

Oh yeah I know I know
 I've walked this old earth for 55 years
  and I guess I have my little store
   of anger and bitterness
which I carry on my back
 like that guy
  in the old fairy tale
and precious friends hid in death's
 dateless night—them in my medicine bag as well
  until like the sun we go under the earth—

But to resume my tale
 I played my lousy flute
  round the island a while
went down to McDonells sat in a stupor
 read the funnies in *The Province*
  after an hour and a half
   dug out my pen, and scribbled the story
felt a lot better
 nodded "good nite" to the guy in the corner
  who seemed to be writing a novel—
Pulled on my work hat
 and started off down Robson

There on the corner
 outside the library

a group of teenagers
  "Want a poem for a penny?"
a beautiful but overweight black girl
  the focus of the group
    with a bunch of roses in her hand
      shouts at me
"Fuck off! Get the fuck out of here!"
I say
  "Have a nice day, lady"
    and cruise up the street
shocked, terrified, in the summer heat.

I put down my hat
  and start to play my flute
    overblowing all the high registers
      in disquietude.

Along come these teenagers
  cruising in a phalanx
    and the same lady
      with the red roses
bends down and picks up my hat
  I wait for her to tip all my poems
    and my pennies out on the sidewalk—
But that's not what happened—
  She walks down the street
    carrying my hat leaving me speechless
      as I watch it go
        off into the distance
and I keep playing my flute
  there's not much else to do
    and I wonder
in what garbage can
  I'll find my hat

"If you want it, come and get it"
  She stops and turns to me
    so with my flute in my hand
      I walk down to where she's standing
She raises it in ritual benediction
  I bow down to take it
    "God be with you!" she blesses me

"And with you too" I answer
and as I say
 some tip of some iceberg or other

The whole episode left me quite blasted
 I don't try to sell no more poems
  that very evening
just walk around, set down my hat
 and play my flute, and know it's all called
  "paying your dues"or something like that
and my tale is a small one
 I've heard of panhandlers
  being cut up
   by razor wielding Nazis
and I'm beginning to get much respect
 for the brotherhood of panhandlers
  demonstrating poverty
   in the world of Virtual Reality

And I myself have not tuned in
 to the CBC since last year
  when they ran me off their architectural forecourt
called the cops on me that time too
 but the cops just laughed and I gave them a poem
Banned from selling poems
 on that bastion of Kanadian Kulchur
  on the people's forecourt
   of the people's media machine
and they've played Mozart to several deaths already

So headed back down Robson
 on my way to bed
ran into Brian Wyvern LeBlanc O'Doyle
 selling sheets of poems
  out of a portafile
His is a winning manner
 and easy confidence
he tells me how he plays the recorder
 "An ancient flute" he tells me
"It doesn't record anything—
 How can you call it a recorder?"
  so we stand talking about flutes

and recorders, He tells me how
   he can follow a line of music.
He's young, with a spark in his eye
 and a twist to his lips
  respectful, well organized
   full of hope, he talks well to people
and gives me a poem
 he wrote it for y'rs truely
  I'm truely honoured by it—
So I tell him my complaint of
 Granville Island and my weird day
  and saying "Good nite"
walk up Burrard Street
 taking off my hat
  and in its place I set
   the hat I nearly lost

I count my change and stop
 at Circle K where the night
  attendants look like they
   could handle themselves
    in any circumstance

They charge me the price of a coffee
 for a cup of hot water
  for my instant ginseng—
a cinnamon bun, wrapped in plastic
 given 20 seconds in the microwave

Over the bridge
 look down on the yachts below
  the expensive toys
   of virtual reality
walk down the side of the bridge
 in the bushes take a ritual pee
come back to my own territory

Under the bridge
 and up the bank
  by my patch of bushes
pull my raincoat out of my bag
 lay it on the ground

and my sleeping bag on top of it
take off my shirt
 and empty my pockets in it
  wrap up the bundle
   lay it by my head
take off shoes and socks
 stuff socks in shoes in case it rains
  put glasses teeth
   and elastic hair tie
    in my old hat

and in my jeans and undershirt
 lay me down to sleep

        A day in the life of a street poet, 1992.

WHAT REALLY HAPPENED

9pm on Robson Street. There I was standing on the corner playing my flute, well perhaps it wasn't on the corner, perhaps it was out side the Little Heidleberg which had just closed down, or up the street under the awning of the International Camera Shop. Yes, I guess that's where it was.

At the beginning of December, and raining, not too heavily, people on the street, and I with my open flute case at my feet, and I'd lit a candle to be christmassy and festive and to encourage people to reach into their pockets—

Well, along comes this native guy. He's wearing a Pink Floyd T-shirt, two faces looking at each other, and he's on crutches, he's lost a leg, but wearing a new pair of jeans tied in a knot under his stump; and with him, a woman, his wife, and an older woman, perhaps his mother. "Strong people they are," that's what I was thinking as I watched them approach—playing music on the street is a great way of people watching, and you play them into your music.

The guy comes up to me and he says:

"We don't have much, but we'd like you to have this," and hands me a styrofoam takeout box. You often get given takeout boxes when busking, and you never know what's in them, and I'd just been given a whole bag of baked goods by the lady in the cafe on Granville Island, so I said:

"Well, I'm OK, thanks, I've got all these baked goods."

He say: "There's steak there . . . and potatoes . . . and zucchini."

My mouth watering, I think, "He really wants me to have this," so I say, "Well, thank you very much."

Then he says, "If you can play some Jethro Tull I'll look in my pocket and see if I can find some change."

I have to admit, "I'm just an old hippy. I play this thing off the top of my head."

We say goodnight and he swings himself on up the wet street, he and the two women.

So I stand there eating the steak and the zucchini and the potatoes—and let me tell you it was tender and it was good and I felt very warm inside, my digestive juices were flowing as they don't often flow. So I licked my fingers and wiped them on my jeans and got out a large piece of quiche, rather crumpled, and added it to the steak and the potatoes and the zucchini, and felt like a bear ready to find a hollow log to crawl into for a long winter's sleep. So down to McD's for a cup of tea to aid the digestion, and then with my umbrella up headed over Burrard Street Bridge, then down under the bridge on the Kitsilano side to an ivy bank that grows there, where, on nights like this when rain is falling, I set down my pack and knapsack, take off my old hat and as I crawl into my bag, set it down by my head, and in it I put my glasses and my teeth (one of the rituals of age is disassembling your face before you go to sleep)

And on my ivy bank I slept so well, like a baby full of his mother's milk—

Once in the night I awoke, a dog is barking, someone is calling it, it must have been morning, but sleep again, and then I wake up, the sky clearing. I think what a good day it will be, reach for my glasses, put them on my nose and peer at the clock on the brewery, "10.53" it read. I must have slept nigh on twelve hours. Put my hand back in my hat—no teeth, "What! No teeth!" I jump up "Someone's stolen my teeth! Some bastard! Some a'hole! Some Mother f'er! Stolen my teeth!"

I search all around in the ivy, stamp through the brambles trying to calculate the pitch and trajectory of my flung teeth, composing stories of Christmas malice.

"Someone's stolen my teeth! Two weeks till Christmas, the best two weeks of the year. I was hoping to make so much money—but now I won't even be able to play my flute. I won't be able to make a penny—Someone's stolen my teeth!

Then after half an hour of fuming I decide: "I'm not going to find them. I guess I'll go to Granville Island, fake it on the flute, maybe people will be charitable."

So I go and stand outside the market—can't play too good, really down, I mean I'm really depressed—play for half an hour not making anything and it's raining again, so I say to myself, "I'll sew some books together, maybe I can sell some books." Get myself some tea and a muffin—my gums are pretty tender but I'm hungry and I always like to eat when I'm depressed. I look in my bag for my sewing kit, needles, thread utility knife which I keep in a zip-up pencil case—but I can't find them—

"They must have thought my money was in it and taken that" and then I imagined their look when they found it was only needles and thread and old pens—so I borrowed needle and thread from Maiwa Hand Dyed Fabrics and sewed a few books together, thought, "well, that's a story," so got out my notebook and wrote it all down, in rather depressed style—but when I had written it, lo, a great weight was suddenly lifted from my mind, I became illuminated with the joyful absurdity of the situation, and then I found my pencil case at the bottom of my shopping bag and realized what had happened: The wonderful taste of the steak and the zucchini and the potatoes had lingered on my teeth. Some animal had been attracted by the aroma, had grabbed them, maybe a rat or a raccoon or the dog I'd heard barking, maybe a crow had flown off with them, perhaps they were hidden in some creatures lair, thinking what a haul it had, what a memento to pass on to its children.

I went out again to play my flute. I was still full of the humour of the event, it seemed like the funniest thing that ever happened to me. All I could think of was, "Wow, this really happened." So I started playing my flute again, and with a little practice found I could play it ten times better without teeth than I could with the bloody things in my mouth. I could play in ways and with expression like I'd never played before, and I even read poetry better without them, though I have to work at every articulation, at least I don't have that baffle in my mouth to block the sound, at least they don't threaten to fly across the room at a dramatic moment, as once they had when I was rehearsing Shylock in Willy the Word's old *Merchant of V.*

So I said to myself: "Who needs false teeth! I might as well accept what I am and stop hiding behind these bits of plastic or whatever—this is the person that I am—so be it—"

1993. Published in *Magic Flute*, 2005.

THE GODS

THE CRAZY GODS WILL CROWN YOU
with their golden speckled laughter
 they ride their elephants
  from the sea
   through the dull cities
 to the highest mountains

They come in robes of ivory
 slippers of parrots feathers
  and polished basalt
   jock straps

The insane gods
 pilgrimage with purpose
  through valleys of honeysuckle
   always asking for you
    in brothels of linoleum
     and markets
      of rust and arborite

Their lips, as they come
 are swollen and sticky
  with the pustules
   of questions
they search among sleepers
 in houses of worn newspaper
in gardens and park benches
 public beaches
  dilapidated trees
   and the dusty scrub
    on the edge of cities

The adventurous mad deities
 are hungry for an eyeful
  of your esteemed person
honourably
 they're gonna catch you
  reverently
   suck your lily-white skin
hug you

49

so to speak
til you turn slowly
 black and blue and yellow
and noises creak
 like old fruit trees
  involuntary
from your barren mouth

The amorous pathetic gods
 are on you
the hungry gods
 lost long ago
  of love, praise, sacrifice
   even worshipers
    are on you
caught like a candy wrapper
 between the parking lot
  and the bridge rail
caught by the pasted store window
 sold out last week
  today full of mutilated posters
they've got you
 the hungry gods
  by the guns of Cambodia
   by the black nursing mother
    of Angola, rifle slung
by the Metal-workers' hall
 and the Fishermans' hall
  the crazy gods have got you
and they suck you cold
 in longing

And the great gods
 all of them
  are coming to ask you
for all the spare change
lying to your muddy mind
 you notice them beside you
  suddenly drinking beer
   with great gulps and burps
and on the bus
 with enormous histories

of how they lost
 their last two jobs
and what they told the boss
 at the end of the shift
  when they were found
 behind the generator shed
  with an empty mickey of rye

and the coffee counter too
 you're sure they're standing
  behind you
   as you slip an extra donut
    into your pocket

you've met them on every corner
 mumbling about past glories
  fighting their way
   through Italy
begging dimes
 for a bus journey
  to a fabulous location
   the place of dreams
    they'll never get to

and the lost gods
 are coming with a question
  a small one
   for a cigaret
    or a match
coming with wet feet
 their heads on fire

and the dilapidated gods
 with memories
  of perfumed temples
slumber in doorways
 nervously watch rainclouds
and examine broken umbrellars
 discarded already
  by urgent mortals
   possibly fixable
  with a piece of bent wire

and the silken gods
 out of tune with angels now
sing lullabies by sooty trees
 sing of the sodden paper
  of their past
   transparent beauty

And the horrendous singing gods
 of wonderful lunacy
are sniffing your footsteps
 in the alleys of the city

the awful gods
 on old goat feet
  and of course
   on gossamer wing
are quite desirous
 of your grass thin person
to pick your mind
 of its fruity imaginings

and the great mad gods
 measure their might
  descend
   in big black boots
    down the glistening
    rainwashed sidewalk
visiting in cafes
 rattling in washrooms
sturdily pouncing
 on your embittered brothers

and the fat senile gods
 will deliciously gobble you up
  roll on your carcass
   in parks of dirty trees

Oh the gods! the gods!
 you forgot them once
  you thought they didn't count
but they know so well
 their ABCs

as they let their fingers wander
  through the yellow pages
    of your sentimental mind

Oh the gods! the gods!
 can you feel their fingers
  tramping
    down the labyrinths?
you wish too late
 y'd safely ate the maps

And the crazy gods
 are dancing
in that well hidden emptiness
 of your defunct imagination

and the dumb gods
 are looking
  in all the wrong places
   you gave them the slip
    when you jumped on the bus
they were searching in cafes
 you hid among tables
  they were queuing for skin flicks
   you sat drinking beer
they were off to the races
 you swam in the ocean

and the spaced-out drunken gods
 are tripping round the galaxy
  looking for a footprint
   of a size eleven boot
    that's yours

and the idiotic imbecilic gods
 are wandering in snowfields
  of a far northern wilderness
   of an even colder planet

and the gods are coming home again
 in whirlwinds of honest stars

singing dusty melodies
 of clouds of incandescent gas

and the watchman of the heavens
 is dreaming out a fantasy
 of strawberry shortcake
 and soft icecream

and strange dark gods are zooming
 on mythologic motorcycles
 making a tour of heaven
 in coffeeshops of lunacy
 and gardens of disgusting peace

and the crazy gods are on you
 masked as cats
 and foul old men

and the gods
 with yellow spittal
 are climbing your carcass
 with spiked boots and ice axe
the prospectors
 of your sacred body
are reaching to the core of things
 polluting y'r spinal fluid
 with their stinking cloudy urine

the kind gods
 have caught you
 hold you in a hammerlock
 press your nose to the cobble stones
 in an alley of stenches
and they kick in your teeth
 in this rainfilled paradise
the honeyed gods are very fierce
 in the pursuit of your despair

and the insane gods
 those little cherubs of crazy
waiting behind a tree
 as you piss against a bush

drinking beer and giggling
 surly at the next table
always at a spot in memory
 rolling and quivering
  behind your bloodshot eyes
possessing with much boisterousness
 your narrow junkfilled skull

and those gods
 all of them
  the whole slimey crew
are jumping down the stairs
 of heaven
  armed with obscenities
   and gorgeous temptations
catch you by the heels
 on the smutty
  concrete sidewalk

And the gods
 you see? you don't?
the recognizable, abstract
 distant, deified fellows
each one a little past his prime
 the slightly corrupt
  but dignified
   and sleepy
    unaccustomed fathers
     of unwelcoming galaxies
out there, beyond the potted plants
 windows, and the prevailing weather
the mutterers of history
 murderers of adolescent dreams
suspect ladies of the star speckled universe
 large hungry slightly slobbering eaters
  of the warm flesh of accident victims
and the casualties of private wars
 in unpronouncable jungles
  under the eye
   of God alone
the great white bloody creature
 the one chairperson of the universe

the gentleman who disposes with glee
your miserable fates in the mud
 of the chance unlucky biosphere
 you inhabit

The crazy gods will crown you
 you drinkers in alleys
the crazy gods will crown you
 you dancers in streets
the crazy gods will crown you
 sleepers on a stained mattress
 the crazy gods
petty thief, scrounger, bagman, nosepicker
 with their golden speckled laughter
blasphemous lumpenprole arselicking
 coffeedrinker
The golden gods . . . *welfare bum, no good*
 remittance man, stranger, stranger
Will mock you . . . *father of brats*
 father of lovely fat greedy babies
 With their crazy gilded laughter
screwer, unfaithful
the Purple Gods *word monger hypocrite*
will bite you
nose mouth and prick
 ribs skin and nipples
With their Golden
 sight smell feel
Speckled *taste hear*
 Laughter

       Hastings Street, 1975.
       Published in *Street Heart Poems*, 1993.

THE HISTORY OF THE SACRIFICIAL LAMB

enuf of that
 and enuf of wotever,
  and wot do we remember?
    the mothers
     the children
the ancient herstories of those words
echoing in the daily news as well
 I cannot write a poim abt that
  there's too much pain
  and too much joy as well
 it's quite beyond the palette
of my palid dictionary.
 Can poitry be so suffused
  with agony and light?

Published in *Trying to Ryt a Poim*, 2000.

BALLAD OF THE MAN OF WAR

My father was a sailor man
   he sailed unpon the seas
he danced among the fishy waves
   so joyful and so free
but he sailed out one shell shocked night
   and he was history

My mother was a good woman
   She prayed on bended knee
and every Sunday after church
   the vicar came to tea
but on day came a telegram
   a widow now she'd be

My bro and I, two little boys
   were playing in the rain
and as she stood inside the door
   her face showed mortal pain
She said, as dryly as she could
   he'd never come again

"Oh Mother dear, oh Mother dear,
my daddy's gone away
 Until the day he comes again
I will no longer play"

"Oh child dear, oh child dear
my head is hurting sore
 I think no more I'll see him come
a striding thru that door"

Oh all the jolly sailor boys
   are sailing with the tide
and stanting waving on the shore
   their popsies and their brides
but when the shells begin to fall
   there ain't no place to hide

So pity the poor widow folk
 and little children sad
who thru no fault of their bloody own
 live in a world gone mad
and one day comes a telegram
 to say they've lost their dad—

PRIDE OF FATHERHOOD

And expect the cornucopia to be burnt
 the full sad eyes of the future
  and the growing darkness
   of children
We know such little parts
 and farts
the echo in my cock
 that catches the song of the thrush
  it being all but winter

We all have our favorite bear poem
 the Leda act, the Silkhie act
for carving totems out of
 face one side bear, one woman
  and of course
   a musty secret smell
and all those childlike faces
 you carry about with you
  but you might have expected it
        then

Hunger you enjoy
 and the travelling eyes
  you c'd feel the dead branch
   and the secret stones
 or spaces inhabitable
  by new tribes
and the conspiracy
 of darkness
  of the swollen earth

We live in sorrowful times
 and the more insistently we dance
  the drum sounds
   with its fateful throbbing
    among the moraines
     of memory

you've felt the sour spittal
 in your teeth
you've seen the shattered windows
 of delight
you were a darling once
 but darlings now
  have gone lumps in my throat

You give stories too
 of fatherhood
y'r laughter yellows to age
 the decayed portions break off
  and blow away in the wind
and then they come a hunting you
 with that awful telephone voice
  they catch you up
   they put you down
but you can't forget your hate

You come
 with the angriest teeth
  of the yellow butterfly
   you say
"Oh Father, rescue me
 from this island of stone hearts"
but it's not me
 y're calling to
  though how you know
   those little secrets
    I'm not likely to forget

but they sold you down the river
 you know
  the whole point has been lost
you were up for sale
 couldn't you guess it
and lock, stock and barrel
 legs, navel and cock
behind y'r back
 under y'r skin

between y'r feet and the ground
  they suddenly declared you
    Sold out!

Out
  in the wide outside
    where the wind
      blows snow and rain
and next summer
  the sun will bleach
    y'r complexion there
in that swampy
  riverside town
    several miles downstream

The journey makes its legs
  quickly
    via the sea
    via the shore
looking for shells
  corners of anger
    anguish of deep water
The kelp brushes the rocks
  the rocks laugh at the waves
    and slowly pay their retribution
and the little stones
  dance with the pounding
    but it's all there
    back in childhood, don't we expect?
and who w'd be proud
  of fatherhood
    we come to make our payments
in the end

My child—my beautiful boy
  who w'd be proud of fatherhood
    if it wasn't for such joy
as you

I c'd call you
  my little warrior maybe

I'll teach you to
   chew on the ears
     of the world
eat the eyes of experience
 for breakfast
to dance on graves
 and laugh in the mouths of judges

When you kiss the arse of the law
 y'll grab its nuts in y'r teeth
   then run down the street
     singing arias
       at the top of your voice
little warrior my hero
 my little spark
   of pure joy
     igniting the hate of the universe

and in the rain
 how come those corners
   of experience?
grim days
 we wait
   with the knowledge
     of incipient hunger
and desire
 a fading leaf

my children, my children
 we all ask questions
   of the future
we exist in the impossible
 what more do we want?
and then, children
 we are only lent some things
   and the others
     derived of fear entirely
       stand up against us

and there is so much
 of standing against us
the territory of rain

and dirty water
foul streets
 and sodden paper
and it's all a shared point
 of borrowed fear

but some I guess
 are well equipt
  have ancient rifles
   hanging on the walls
    stout boots
(that's what we need—stout boots)
 and ancient hungers
  flapping in the wind
and the blood of our last time
 the spaciousness of hunger
  and the stories that are impossible
   the final dance of the wind

and in the specious spheres
 of abundance
  we shuffle our feet
y're laughing
  like a tumbled angel
 the emptiness
   pours its light upon us
  its poverty
   as one might say
    a quantity of radiance
     and nothing else

 lentils we want
our glad days
 gone under
and my children
 what word now
  for your precious joy?
 we've fallen heavily
  on winter

and then we're finished up
 like a good child's
  bowl of porridge
chasing the scraps
 around the bottom
(while Peter Rabbit and his sisters
 run around the top)

and fished up too
 caught in the net
  of readers' eyes
also like a bomber
 laying eggs over Berlin
 or somewhere else
diving through nets
 of searchlights
  and bursting shells

and washed up too
 like a broken fish float
 or a dead seagull
  covered with oil
after a minor accident
 or perhaps just carelessness
  in port

We are all these things
 of course
  and many others
each with its appropriate
 or adventurous tag
 of simile

We run our lives
 like an octopus
  in a treadmill
or a freak show
 sent to entertain the troops
  on a top secret battle front
We have such desires
 for rightness
  and sense of place

we forget the continental drift
 is happening
  every day.

Occupied on a search
 for beauty
dodging the obvious
 lost in meanings
  we might be afraid of seeing
Where we have landed now
 y'r eye
  always the eye of the hawk
  in my direction

I mean to go to birth
 to find meaning
of course
 we hold it all back
  all our love
when it's all a matter
 of springing into this world
  quite untidily
   you know

but can you forgive the child
 for being born
especially
the child
 that was yourself
  that dragged you by the heels
into the future

and arithmetically
 you plot y'r progress
  in a limp
   across the parking lot
that reaches from here
 to the water's edge
and down under the water
 climbing the further shore
but we are still at this side
 steadfastly dragging out feet.

I take you
through such declensions
 of my living, and yours
I've introduced you
 to my wives and children
I've lined them up for you
 and also drank your beer
  that I'll admit

We've shared patches
 of sunlight
and stood together
 under leaky umbrellas
You say
 "We're reaching into space"
  you call for spirits from the grave
   maybe

but then
 at this momentary lapse
  of history
maybe you'll find somewhere
 by an abandoned
  cash register
among crushed paper
 cream containers
cigaret packets
 full of ashes
an isolated ashtray
 in a distant cafe

by ill-conceived donuts
 where music moves
  like swarming bees
and the dimensions
 of the coffee counter
  are geographically notorious—
a postulate
 of final comfort
among the concrete
 and polished plastic

1974–1975, *Remember those years?*

67

TEENAGE POEM

Under the bushes
among the sticks
 and the flies
bodies naked in the woods
 and the mist growing in the woods
  the cold of winter's night
   and body's heat

unnatural acts
 quite naturally
  crawl away and hide in the woods
say
 "This is my flesh"
  we flow out into night
   like the tune from the juke box
in a cafe across the street
 as a door opens
  and a couple goes in
or comes laughing out

 Well we've described ourselves
so many times in each others' eyes
 and on solitary nites
  in the bushes
 the pulsating hotnesses of swelling flesh
  feeding on desire

love's own attitude
 white limbs
  under the bushes
flow and melt away

 and sorrow's own untidy garden
but where
 do you find us
now among the trees?
 the apple trees are flowering
  red and white

it's all bees' world
here wherever
and whenever
in the dust

2001.

NO CUNTREE FOR OLD MEN?

We bury ourselves in language
  and when we come to dig ourselves out
all we find
  are a few small bones
  gnawed on
by little animals
  with lots of little squeaking
    hairless babies
and naked tails

  and in the loving darkness
    of the dead of night
you whisper the ambiguous words
  of history
    into my sleepy ear

and your laughter
  fills the universe
where suddenly among the stars
  you build the city of love for us again

the concrete dictionary
  of human foibles
    dancing, singing, crying, fighting,
      kissing
  all mapped out
    by the sweaty shape of our desire

  but what are our desires?
just to be wrapped again
  in comfortable flesh
    to take the loveliness
shining through a wayward eye
  and hide it deep
    within our anxious corporality

Who knows
  as history knew us
  a puppet on a string
"Dance" they said "dance, Godamit"

"Kick your heels
  til the house of straw
    comes tumbling down"
  well, we danced our dance
   and the fiddler fiddled
and nonchalantly chewed his gum

You wrote the book of it
 you called it 'love'
you wrote the history
 of my desire
  in many different
   coloured inks
and buried my dreams
 in the compost pile
out behind the holly tree
 to make the garden sweet

 now I'm a lexicographer
in the language of desire
  cartographer
of those dark and dreamy places
 the fecund swamps
  of our aging bodies
 a lepidopterist, I collect
Vocabularies
 full of rich smells
  the finding and the joining
   of the night

the whole universe
 is dusty with pollen.
Here our orgasmic wonderland
where we are tourists
 or perhaps pilgrims
  you could say
of this ancient erotic landscape

and your bones each night
 sang their sweet song to me—

But wot do you do with old poets?
with their language
  like rusty razor blades?

wot do you do with old poets
with their lies
  they are so good describing
    what is no longer here
      nor never was

Old poets
  with decaying bodies
    smelling of mildew, dry rot
      skunk cabbage and rotting fish

standing by the hiway
  like signposts to a past
    that fled, laughing, away

the muse
  like a decrepit crone
    still whispers
and the old poet still giggles
  at her jokes

but the old poet
  draws the punchline
    out to eternity
and who's to wait around these days
  for his retelling

the old poet has undoubtedly seen
  better days
    he'll tell you that himself
the blood ran hot once
  where now's all aches and pains

the old poet sits
  in an all nite coffee shop
feeling quite sorry for himself
  just like young poets do
unless they're the kind

the Goddess looked upon
 and smiled

But the old poet can still delight
 in the spark in a young girl's eye.

"The whiplash rain
 upon the window
  of the fast food cafe
 where I drink my tea
  and scribble
There are so many good poets out there
 who needs another me?"

"let me hold you
  in my arms
let me taste again
  your charms."

Published in *Trying to Ryt a Poem*, 2001.

THE BALLAD OF RONNY WALKER

For Ronny Walker 1912–1992

Beware of old men
and their rusty old poems

and Ronny Walker
  the one-eyed Old Bastard on Pine Street
dying alone in his junk filled house
  the water turned off
as the pipes burst during the cold spell
  while he was in the hospital
    after his heart attack
or was it pneumonia? the rumors vary.

He has so much highly valued junk
that to move it all
  and find the plumbing problem
    is beyond capability.

He has collected all this stuff
  tools, books,
    clocks that run backwards
      records, lamps, second-hand
      building materials,
it seems
  as a sheet anchor
    against Death.

To move him
  to take his stuff,
    would pillage all his purposes.

A lonely dying man
  in a house filled with junk.

And I still have the condom
  he gave Briar
    saying all she needed
      was a good fuck
      and a bottle of brandy

her, with her back broken
 dying of cancer.

And he told me
 how once he woke up
  to find her in bed beside him
but he couldn't help her
 and he cried as he said it
"I couldn't help her,
  I couldn't help her!"

Those two had a real love
 each so sure of rejection
  in the world of people,
and I drove them to the beach
 I, her chauffeur
  he, her gallante.

And the day she died
 I borrowed 20 bucks from her dad
  and went down town to find him
take him for a drink

And it was Bathtub Days
 although I didn't know it
  had forgotten, didn't register
till I came to Commercial Street
 around the gigantic
  Pepsi and Coke cans
   20 feet high
    filled with hot air
and the breakdancers
 and the kids
  on BMX bicycles
doing their tricks to the raucus music
 pumped out by the CHUB truck

And there was Ronny Walker
 twisted cane, velvet jacket,
  button saying "Be Rude"
long white hair and beard
 and his one sharp eye.

I could not even tell him
 for the noise in the street
  so I took him to the Palace
   set a beer before him
and went for Jim the Mechanic
 and a few other spirits
  told them "Briar got promoted"

So we sat around a laden table
laughed and cried
 and then I rowed my boat
  over to the island
never did get drunk.

Oh Ronny Walker
 y'r going down to death
  with all your bitter memories

And today I left him
 pissing off his back porch
  and saying
"Do you know Lewis Mumford?
 the one who wrote
  The Culture of Cities.
He said 'When you can no longer
 piss off your back porch
  it's time to move on.'"

So I said
"I need a piss too"
and unzippered
 and got it out
and pissed off the pathway
 into the snowbank
  (March 3rd, late snow)
which covered a pile
 of assorted junk
  in his yard-space

And Ronny
 pissing off his back porch
  it's not yet time
   to move on.

"I'm short of breath" he says
"short of breath."

And leaving him alone
 with no water
the hot plates on the stove
 turned on for heat
holes in the windows
 where kids had pitched rocks in
  surrounded by empty boxes

his seemed a very
 temporary establishment
no water even to wash himself
 even to flush the toilet

An old man
 at the end of his tether
come home to die
 in the accumulations of a lifetime

and his truck won't start
 and the battery's dead.
Someone stole his extension
 and most of his tools,

And someone else will probably come
 and take him to a more hygienic place
  so he'll die among scurrying women,
but I won't blow the whistle on him.

Has not a man, like a beast,
 the right to choose
  where he wants to die?

Oh Ronny, die quickly
before they move you out of here.
Don't let them break your spirit
 before they let you go.

3rd March 1991

THE DEATH AND APOTHEOSIS OF RONNY WALKER

Two old men lived in a city
on the western edge of things
One was a pirate
he was the Mayor and waved a plastic sword
he was a realtor and a pirate too
he was a good fellow
I've no harsh words for him

The Other was a carpenter
he had one eye
long white hair
a silken beard
and a wicked turn of phrase
He called himself
'The Old Bastard on Pine Street'
at the college on the hill
they called him Diogenese

They are both dead now
wherever they might be
died within a few months of eachother

And the Pirate said he'd fought
in the Battle of Britain
and the One Eyed Old Bastard
he'd been to Spain—he said
but he lost his eye at cards
someone was cheating
though whose to know the truth of it

Well I bought him his last beer
and you can believe everything I say
and got him into the Oxy
one last time before he died

The Oxidental Pub
by the railroad tracks
Moose, Elk and Cariboo and Wolf
gazing down on the drinkers

They called it the Oxidental
'cos back one hundred years
they wouldn't let no Celestials in
it was that kind of town then
back in the old days
though they toiled and died together
in the coal-dust underground

In that same historic spot
under a buffalo's pontifical gaze
many years ago
Ronny stood up and pissed in someone's beer
to enforce a philosophic point
while the unlucky drinker
was visiting the can

and the women all up and left
and he got barred for life—for life

That summer before he died
I saw him coming down the hill
Old man of eighty
leaning on his crooked stick
"Hi Ron" I say
"Go fuck y'rself" his usual reply
"I c'd do with a drink" he says
"Let's go in, get one" I say
"I can't, I'm barred"
I knew that as well as he
"Come on we'll try anyway"
always the trouble maker I am
particularly if my arse is covered—

Well, we went in, sat down
the place had grown some carpets
lost a few heads
more tastefully decorated indeed
since the last time I was there

So the waitress comes over
"And what will you two gentlemen be having?"
"Gentlemen, gentlemen—" little did she know

then she comes back
and very politely says
"Is y'r name Ronny Walker?"
"Yes"
"A customer round the other side
tells me that you're barred for life"

Well, I chirp in
"That's about something
that happened years ago
this place has changed hands
five times since then
Look it's a hot day, he's an old man
we're just going to drink one beer"

"Well—alright" she says
and serves us very graceful like—
So we get our beer at the Oxy
for Life, for Death

Soon Ronny Walker's dead
and he died with a smile on his face

Well, I know
I saw him just before he died
he knew he was going
could no longer walk down the hill
into town—
"awful short of breath"

He sat in his yard
surrounded by his junk
I brought him a six-pack
of OK Springs Larger
we each had a beer
then we stashed the rest
by a pile of books
beneath a piece of carpet

"I'm bleeding from my arsehole
the doctors want to open me up
cut a piece out"

that's what he tells me
as we drink our beer

Well, that last time
at the end of summer
I walked up stairs
found him lying in his bed
playing with himself
saying goodbye
to his earthly pleasure
to his Garden of Delight

he covered it up
and we talked a while
he sent me downstairs
to get the rest of the beer
but someone else
had gotten there before me
but I found us a bottle
with some Ginseng Brandy in it
and in our talking was a gentle finality
He told me how he wanted
to once more see his daughter
I said I'd try to find her
on my travels up country

That night I called again
before catching the ferry
I found him lying there
just as I'd left him

"Will you be OK if I go now?"
"Do you need to ask permission?"
"See you when I get back"
but for both of us
it seemed to lack conviction

Then I hitch hiked up the hiway
up through Grand Forks
tried to find his daughter
but her number was unlisted
and I'm not so very sure

I had her name down right
though I tried all the combinations

and when I got back he was dead
and his inlaws
were tossing out his stuff

and Jane said
"Where's Ronny Walker?"
"In Heaven,
bullshitting with St Peter"

A couple of weeks later
walking by the railroad
I met this junkfood preteenager
twelve or thirteen

"I know your name" he says "It's John"
"No, it's not"
"Y're Old Man Walker"
"No, I'm not. Ronny Walker's dead"
"I know" he says "I killed him"

"No, you didn't
He died with a smile on his face"

"Yes, I killed him
I beat him up
I was robbing his place
and I killed him"

"No, you didn't
He died with a smile on his face"

"I killed him
I killed him"
the kid kept saying
as I walked away
By the time I'd left
he believed his boast himself
God save us from the evidence
of such kids!

But let us turn the clock back
Well, the Old Pirate
he was mayor for years
in his cocked hat
skull and crossbones
and his faded red jacket

but times change
and a technocratic woman
a funding consultant
comes on the scene
a growing city
stepping stone to politics

and the Old Pirate
rests on his laurels

and that lady
brings a more aggressive stance
to city hall
have to clean the place up
get the bilaws active

Now, Old Ronny was the worst
most acquisitive pack rat
you'd ever meet
filled up his yard
with every kind of junk
that he could buy or swap or scrounge
intent on spending
the last of his wealth
before his heirs could have it
and full of wonderful projects
to do with all the stuff

A man of powerful hates he was
and eighty years old
and his one eye the sharpest
that you ever saw

Thus it transpired that the city
decided that it must do something

with the Old Bastard's property
he'd been giving them grief for years
with the lane they wanted to widen
to get more traffic down the back alleys
and the broken sewer line
washing into his back yard
He's been up there through the years
calling those suited fellows
every kind of unprintable name
offending their precious dignity
Oh how they stood
on their precious dignity

So the bilaw department
gets its rear end in gear
swoops down upon him
like a buzzard on a roadkill

they sent him ultimatums
go before the court
but the court date got shifted
so the old man never got
to bullshit with the judge

a new kind of shell game
shifting court dates
on an ancient one-eyed carpenter

Well they got a court order
"Clean up your yard
or the city will hold an auction
to pay for the removal"

That's what the order said
I know because I read it
But court orders
w'd you believe it
are open for interpretation

The City found an auctioneer
walked him round the old man's yard
and asked the guy

"Do you want any of this?"
"Nah, nah" he says
he doesn't want
to be bothered with it

So that's how they held their auction
I saw that happen too
and the contract was already signed

And that same morning
the very same morning that they held
their phony auction
Hub City Paving comes
with its mechanical grabber
and a couple of dump trucks

Oh yes it's legal
but wots legal just ain't justice
and when it comes to money
who gives a shit for justice
you can quote me
on that line of poetry

so they smash it all up
roofing material
double glazed windows
furniture
old stereos
china dishes
smash it all to pieces
glass all over the place
then pick it all up
with their mechanical grabber
load it into trucks
take it to the dump

Two days it took them
the bilaw cops
standing round
with their walki-talkis
and the old man cursing at them
spitting on their boots

cursing the woman
from the bilaw office
"What was it Lear said to Goneril?"
he asks me, it was something unrepeatable
then "I feel tired
I'm going in to sleep"

I say to the bilaw officer
"You'll be lucky if he doesn't
have a heart attack
and croak right in his sleep
This town would be mud
from one end of the country
to the other"

but he comes out
much rested
in a couple of hours
to curse again

And a neighbour
he comes down the road
sucking on his pipe
"Why are they doing this
to old Ron?" he asks

and another neighbour
comes and says
"I heard it on the radio
they're gonna charge you
ten thousand bucks"

but remember
it was a supposed complaint
from a supposed neighbour
that gave them the legality
for this iniquity

Well, I was witness
and Wendy came
and took the pictures

and they got me too
the short arm of justice
the long arm of the law

and when the bill came
I wrote out the story
and took it to Victoria
to the Ombundsperson's office

they sent a letter back
not their jurisdiction
being a civil matter
but should get legal council
before it was added to the taxes
as he could lose his home—they said
—that's what the city wanted
I got to be thinking

but Legal Aid told us
they couldn't foreclose
on a pensioner's home
they'd collect from his widow
the ten thou' with interest
after he departed

I thought this for sure
w'd bring him to his grave
but he didn't seem put out
he lived for a good fight

just went on buying junk
and books and stoves and stereos
beds and cabinets
thrown out by the hospital
buying with a vengeance
stacking all the stuff
up in his yard again

one day I said to him
"I'm not helping you no more
buy any other stuff
you've got no need of it"

there was no longer anywhere
to stack it in his house

the kitchen was piled high
right up to the ceiling
with empty boxes
brought back from the likker store
all one on top of t'other

he planned to pack his stuff in them
he had so many projects
collecting all this stuff
and using it in any
unconventional fashion
to build his retaining wall
where the lane was falling in his yard
or insulate his house
or cover the broken windows
where the kids had pitched rocks in

So his yard was filled with junk again
boxes of books and records
of the kind you wouldn't want
ever to listen to—with carpet pulled over them
and his beer stashed beneath
he'd lie in the sunshine
on a hospital lounger
happier than a pig in shit

One time I came to visit him, he said
"It's the Sally Ann Antique Auction
let's go!"
So down to the Salvation Army Citadel
(that's what they call their church)

well, it wasn't much of a story
the Sally Ann auction
anything more than ten years old
they'd declare to be antique
cheap aluminum teapots
they advertise as 'sterling'

and they'd brook no complaints
being in a good cause an' all

Ronny buys junk by the boxful
his motto "I'll take the lot!"
he liked to spend where others saved
to demonstrate
his power of money

And then came up this suitcase
with kilt, sporan, tamoshanter
and wool socks, army issue
all full of moth-holes
hardly held together

"Hey, look at that Ron,
bid on that!"
giving him a big nudge
in the spirit of the occasion

I see him in my minds eye
all dressed up
in his kilt and his sporan
nothing underneath
stomping through the town
with his twisted cane
and the sharp edge
and the gentle edge of his tongue

Well, it comes to the pay-out
can't find his checkbook
He's looking through his pockets
and all through his knapsack
while these rapacious women
rummage through his boxes
picking out his treasures
to carry off
to their second-hand stores

He turns to me and says
"Give me your checkbook"
I say "Ron, I can't pay for all your stuff"

"No, no, give me a blank check"
He takes one
and with his pen
inks out the numbers
so the computer can't read them
writes it for four hundred bucks
signs his name and puts his address on it
and gives it to the woman at the till

We load up his stuff
in someone's truck
benches from the college
he stacks them in his yard
all adds to the glorious pile

Now a few days later
I was over in Vancouver
down in Chinatown
buying a bag of steam buns
to bring home to the kids

Had to use the bank machine
lots of money in the bank
but it wouldn't give me nothing

tried all the other bank machines
they all said I was broke
I scraped together all my change
went home to the Island

next day was at that bank door
as soon as it was open
His check had gone through my account
the computer read the numbers
although they were blacked out
and nobody had bothered
to look at the signature

Well, I guess the check
bounced right back on the Sally Ann

who were none too pleased
poetic justice
for those 'sterling' teapots
and when I told Ronny
we had a good laugh
but he paid them back
all in his own good time

And Ronny told me stories
of dubious historicity
how as a young lad
they took him back to England
to visit his relations
hobnobbing with the Prince of Wales
and with Old Queen Mary
how he met Ghandi
wonderful tales of the poor boy
from the colonies,
all slightly apocraphal

He told me
how he was the second man on the island
to sign up with the carpenters union
and how they kicked him out
he wouldn't toe no party line
and how he stole
his best friend's wife
their few good years
before it all went sour

and all the homes
how they were built
who lived in them
and the gardens they had planted
and the women
he remembered them all
all their kindness
as we walked down the street
into town

and how he built the sculpture
in Pear Tree Gardens

a cubistic Elvis
ten feet high
how he mad the forms
for the Frenchman who designed it
and cast it in concrete
and still is it standing

But the tale of Ronny
and the Royal Canadian Mounted
well it's like this

So he has all this stuff in his yard
carparts and tools
and anything anyone might want
So kids come in and steal his stuff
and adults come in too
and help themselves
Well he had it all
but it served no one
so you get the idea
by night his stuff
would grow legs and walk
right out of his yard
w'd liberate itself
make itself useful
get itself recycled

Old Ronny was quite jealous
of his property
w'd never lend a thing to anyone

one night
he was sitting in his kitchen
drinking with Tim
the Reverend's son
a known drunkard
pothead and petty criminal
well known to the police
a gentle guy
a very reverend's son
who never did grow up
just looking for the kingdom of Heaven

like his daddy told him
"become as little children"
that other carpenter
had said

So they're in the kitchen
drinking down a beer
when they hear this noise
someone ripping off the yard again
Get out and holler
and the old man phones the cops

"Get y'r arses over here"
I can hear him shouting
"What the hell do we pay you for"
he never was respectful
never was his habit

so after twenty minutes
the cops come in their cruiser
Ronny told me the whole story
I'd a hard time believing it
but by subtle interrogation
got the same tale Tim
for a poet's business is Justice

They come with their flashlight
shining in his eye
He tells them to put it out
in some kind of language
They come into his kitchen
hit him with the flashlight
breaking the skin
above his brow

then they throw Tim
who is wrestling with the flashlight
off the Old Bastard's porch
take them to the lock up
hospitality of Her Majesty
and charge them in the morning
with assaulting a police officer

Well I heard it all
'cos Ronny had to go to court
and again the date is shuffled
He's late for his court date
so I go and find him
walking down the hill
for his morning beer
he seemed to have forgotten

The judge and he swop witticisms
respectfully, but sharp
and then the judge laughs
and says "Case dismissed"
Ronny wants to tell his story
but the judge bangs his hammer down
he doesn't want to hear it

and Ronny starts on at the Council
about some incident in history
about the MLAs mother
Ronny was in love with once
and he would have married her
but he didn't have a job
back in the dirty Thirties

Tim never did show up
though he had every good intention
so they swore him out a bench warrant
put his picture in the paper
for good citizens to turn him in
for good hard cash
they caught him after the old man
was dead
so he didn't have a witness
and gave him a month in clink

But back to the court house
and out the door
We went to the Globe
the lawyers' girly bar
featured by Lowery
Malcom of that name

when he stopped once for a ferry
off to Gabriola
an a grey October's day

the place was being renovated
dark and cavernous
full of sawdust and two by fours
but there weren't no dancing girls

from across the dim room
someone sent over
a tableful of beer
Someone that none of us knew
so that's the story
of Ronny and the Mounted

All winter, spring and autumn
Ronny would sit in his bathroom
listening to the radio
sitting on the toilet
said it was the warmest place
sipping ginseng brandy
always three radios
on three different stations
chattering away
in the kitchen, bathroom
bedroom

When he was sick that time
pneumonia I guess it was
taken in and nursed
by a Lady of the Night
all his pipes got frozen
and the plumbing burst
the stink from the bathroom
got so bad it clung to yr clothing
all the day after

I found a box of baking soda
in the kitchen cupboard
tipped it down the toilet
took a couple of buckets

went down to the Cat Stream
the little creek across Pine Street
drew some cold clear water
and threw it down the toilet

Ronny liked that
he told his neighbour
some kind of minister
Mennonite I think
and he said
"Now there's a Christian for you"
but I said
"No just a guy
with a sense of smell"
that Hooker was the Christian
if any were about the place

and Ronny wouldn't let me
touch his plumbing problem
he'd been a construction foreman
and knew much too well
the kind of job I'd do

The kitchen was full of boxes
a naked red hot hotplate on for heat
perched on a kitchen chair
hardly room to move
from the back door to the stairs
A clock on the wall
with back to front numbers
hands travelling backwards
widdershins they call it
in the witches language
but taken from a barber's shop
so the shavee could see the time
and kittens tumbling among the boxes
I was always surprised
the whole place
didn't go up in smoke and flames
a Viking funeral
for the old man

If I'd been the one
to have found him dead
I think I might just
have set the whole place ablaze
but I guess they gave him
a proper Catholic funeral
He'd swapped his soul already
for breakfast at their soup kitchen

but he loved his cats
gently mothered them
and the mother brought her kittens
to his bed
they slept all over him
till he was hopping
with the fleas

Slowly every morning
he'd walk down the hill
he wouldn't stop to rest
he'd stop to peruse the landscape

He c'd tell you all the tales
all the love of every house
of the gardens
and the women, now old
he'd known in the days of their beauty

Always he talked so gently
to the old women
he saw their beauty shining still
but younger women he'd tease
something terrible
and make them blush
with the language of his tongue

He had a card from Hell
sent by the Mayor
to The Old Bastard on Pine Street
he'd proudly show it
to anyone he met

pointing to the Norwegian stamp
stuck in the corner

He w'd walk up to the crest of Albert Street
tap his stick
on the concrete barricades
showing how they protect the cars
cornering too fast
from flying off the edge
but the human pedestrians
got no protection whatever

"I've been up to City Hall
so many times
to tell those cacksockers
to move the barricade
just a couple of feet
but they never do it"

After he died
by some divine miracle
or burocratic decision
the barricades moved themselves
between the road
and that bit of pavement
marked off
with a painted line
for human beings
and their dogs
to walk along

Then down the hill he went
to bull shit in the Superette
maybe buy a case of dogfood
for an evening snack
down to the Sally Ann
to buy up records, books
an old computer
in an enormous console
from some antediluvian
government office
anything and everything

that would sit in boxes
by the door
with "Sold Ronny Walker"
marked in big black letters

Sometimes he was barred
thrown out of the Sally Ann
told never to come back
his language offended
the young girls
of the staff
His tongue
could turn
like the weather
in anger
and impatience
and like a child
he wanted
to be the centre
of attention

then down the road
to the Mall
and the likker store
to fill up his pockets
with miniature bottles
of Brandy and Vodka
and to Wendy's
where he'd sit
hold court with Bill
who was ten years his senior
and an old AA man
yet he called Ron
"The Old Fellow"

One day Bill said
"The Old Fellows died"
he'd heard it from the women
at the Sally Ann office
holding a funeral
for "Walker"

I ran up the hill
saying under my short breath
"You Old Bastard
you've done it to me"

the last time I'd seen him
I got pissed off
at his language
and imperious manner
hadn't seen him in a while
I was his friend
not his social worker

went up to his place
it was locked
banged on his door
couldn't hear no radio

went round to his neighbour's
sure he'd given me the slip
found him sitting drinking tea
playing with her kids

"Hi Ron" I said
"am I glad to see you!
I'd heard that you were dead
seems some slight exaggeration"

"I hadn't noticed it" he said

Down the bottom of the hill
a little square of concrete
on which grew a red leafed Japanese maple
a most beautiful little tree
surrounded by a wooden bench
on all four sides

In winter this spot
would catch the sun's low rays
and in summer the old men
would sit here whittling carvings

Well, this developer
by name of Marshall something
wants to turn the area
into some kind of
'people place'
a sort of euphemism
kind of like the
'parkway'

He buys up the old store
next to the little square
divides it up
with balconies
into three levels
of little shoplets
decides he doesn't like
the old men who sometimes
drink too much
whose language sometimes
gets a little bit intemperate

so he phones up the bilaw office
gets some verbal permission
moves in his strong-arm
people sitting on the seats
as his wrecking crew
start to turn them into splinters
kicking off the people
and laughing

We're down there
sitting on what's left
while a deputation of the local boys
John Rose as spokesperson
is up in City Hall
and a girl from the newspaper
an apprentice journalist
comes by and checks the scene

Along come his carpenters
their tools around their waists
come a-cursing at us

Fucking Cocksuckers
one shouts at us
overbrimming with violence

Now there's a difference
in tone and intent
though perhaps not in vocabulary
between swearing and cursing
to swear is to embellish
with obscenities or profanities
to curse
is to commit to hell
or to throw the perversities
of the act of love
in someone's face

Well this guy complains
his wife had heard bad language
casually employed
then he calls us "Fucking cocksuckers"
readying his mind
to take a swing at us

So the little tree has gone
and as the poet says
"Only God can make a tree"

The Lady Mayor
had a bench installed
an ugly thing of concrete
and two by fours
but no one ever sat on it
and it's gone too
and Marshall wotsit's people place
can't hardly make the rent
the wrong side of the hiway
though he'll never lose
a goddam buck himself
and the Media
and the *Nanaimo Magazine*
and the *Nanaimo Times*
he got them all in line

gotta keep the city clean
make it into a 'People Place'

But someone wrote
on the risers of the steps
'Ronny Walker Steps'
they lead down to Lois Lane
a helipad for Superman
who's going to come and save us all
from Bad Guys
Atom Bombs
Pollution and unscrupulous developers
and old men who like to drink too much
and rowdy, irreverent poets

Well they got me too
the Madam Lady Mayor
takes a walk round the South End
South Central Nanaimo
tells the citizens
"No, we can't do nothing
about the industry
the plywood mill
rumbling and clanking
all the night—
No, you can't have no walkway
over the new upgraded hiway
there's nothing we can do
about the railroad
and the tank cars

But w'll make you clean up
y'r backyards
remove the old cars
they bring down the tone
of the neighbourhood
so much
and the blackberries
We've got laws against blackberries

The Rich don't know it
but the 'junk' the poor own

is often their only wealth
but the Rich write the rules
a truck full of spare parts
on the hoof as one might say
is a very real investment
a blackberry vine
a garden full
of Jerusalem Artichokes
Well, they got all mine
and sent me a bill
for one thousand bucks
for my contempt
of the god almighty bilaw department
and my standing by watching
as they despoiled Ronny Walker

They taught me to think
in obscenities
but I know which way the cookie crumbles
and who gets the crumbs
and know that Ronny
is sitting with St Peter
Bullshitting
at the doors of Heaven
sipping ginseng brandy
laughing at the pomposity
of the petty burocrats
of this human plane
and the kangaroo courts
of city hall
who've never understood
the first principles of justice
and never had the wisdom
to listen to a poet
or a crazy one eyed old bastard
who might show them
how their judgement
is tainted with the smell of bucks
and seemliness
as they want to make this old coal mining town
into the chosen destination
of migrant yuppie populations

and give the place
an up scale aire
sweep all the humans
homo ridicularis
under the astroturf

but they've yet
to exorcise
the ghosts

Published in *Death and Apotheosis of Ronnie Walker*, Dec. 1992.

PECUNIA NON OLET

You borrowed us from the sea
 indeed it was so glad of us
  and hid us like a crab
   under a stone

and then you lent us for a while
 to the rocky shore
  to mud bank and tide pool
to the estuaries where the salt and sweet
 flow into each other like lovers
  in the fecund, sunfilled shallows

You lent us to the hills
 already green with every kind of life
  with butterflies
   dragonflies
    cockroaches
     slugs
and a thousand kinds of patient plants
 sustaining life
  and termites, mould and fungus
   digesting rot

borrowings
 burrowings
  broken wings
   where the raven sings

but we sit around
 and drink a pot of beer
  you ask
"What is the hundred thousandth name
 for God?"
  and she:
"and what are the steps
 in the dance of God?"
the simple steps
 where we stumbled
  as we tried to trace the figure
   of the universe?

Is it so important to know the answer
  once you've asked the question?
and know the answer is contained
  in all about you?

We are haunted by
  those imperial eagles
while the humble weeds
  breath quietly for us
and those ultimate robber barons of the sky
  soar above our heads, and we say:
  "How the spirit soars!"
forgetful of the sweet
  and bitter earth

forgetful of moss and mould
  and the penetrating roots
  of hardy weeds
  bitter to the taste
  spiney, thorny, fibrous
matter of fact flowers
  matter of fact windfluff of seed
those pioneers of the empire of plants
  high on a rockface
  of flowering briefly
  in a crack in the concrete
  of a runway
  built for bombers
  which darken the sky like eagles
  roar from horizon to horizon
their graffiti marking the sky
with their oil-slick—
  those fucking eagles!

But the forests
  the Great Forests of the Earth
  they will grow up, despite us
  despite our hunger
  and the size of our darkness
It is they that sustain the earth
  we tear them apart
  but they will come back

though we find ourselves
  without their sustenance
they will come back too slowly to save us

Our world is the world of people
 of money, the only reality
  the ultimate abstraction
while we suck at the forest
 like a hungry child
  at the breast of her dying mother
Our money moves round this Earth
 at the speed of light
  it sucks like a hungry mouth
  of a lamprey or hagfish
 wherever it finds sustenance

PECUNIA
 the only reality—the ultimate abstraction
 the symbol of civilized man—
  NON OLET
 it never stinks
unlike our bodies
 unlike the compost pile
 unlike the salmon
bearing its load of nutrient
 up from the rich ocean
  to die by its birthing stream
  high in the mountains
money does not decay
 when everything decays
  money does not stink
it is as cold as the penis of Satan
it is as cold as the grave of God

 and then that old devil
who is he but God himself
who digs a hole for us and buries us
 under the apple trees?

We think we are deserving
 of the everlasting beneficence
  of the universe

of the forest, of the river, of the sea
 our beneficence is that we will rot
  be eaten by little creatures
 be explored by the roots of bitter herbs
quietly unlocking the bonecase of our desire

and the devil
 the horned goat man
  and the scarlet woman
dance unstumblingly
 in the figure of the Dance of God
and drink of the Cup
 of the laughter of God
  sit down, tell tales
   of the foolish history
herstory of self important man
 and woman too
of the fatuous self importance
of the unruly children of Adam and Eve
 (I say Adam first because A comes before E)
  but the difference is all the same.

You may call Earth a "Goddess"
 but that doesn't let you off the hook
Indeed Earth is no more a woman
 than God is man
It's just a convenient
 and inaccurate way
  of looking at things
   through our mortal eyes
as we have to give things form
 and name, to talk of them

and God and the Devil dancing together
 are the shape of the space
  of the eternal flux
   between us and the rest of the universe
between our conceiving mind
 and all that is so well defined
  beyond the permeable membrane
  of our consciousness

all that fecund chaos
 the shape of dusty ever living space

and the idea of God
 is somehow more powerful
  more complex more enduring
than the cunning solutions
 of erudite men
  sitting in studies
   writing their books
    of how they found the answer
   to this and to that
    under a stone like a little crab

for the idea of God is the total summation
 of all the unanswerable questions
the total unease
 we feel in the face of the universe
and her story
 which will ultimately
  count us as nothing.

But as saith the Old Black Book
 God planted a Garden East of Eden
and what sort of garden
 did the Old Guy plant?
a total community of all living things
 in their harmony
  which was the Harmony of God

 But God planted also
  the seeds of understanding
 of restlessness and desire for comfort
  in the long winter nights
   of the reign of ice
these seeds he planted
 like the eggs of a tapeworm
  in the secret mind
   of one of his creatures

And the Garden with its Harmony
 became a dream

for the Cat was out of the Bag
and the children of Eve
 a discord in that harmony
 were out of the Garden
  to toil in the heat of the sun

AN ELEGY RITTEN ON A GREYHOUND BUS TRIP TO THE STROLL OF POETS IN ED'TOWN AND BACK VIA CALGARY—

Seems like orl poits wen thay reach a sertin age and liv mor in the past than in the present, being ful of feyer nd dred of the futur, tend to get longwinded nd rite eligies or 4tits or cantos—stuf lik that so 4give me mi selfindullgnce, it's lik biological

"Do not tell me of the wisdom of old men but rather of their folly"
　　—T.S.Faber (I ain't old, but I'm older than he were wen he writ that)

SO WE PREPARE FOR NIGHT
 for the dark night
and say
 "is this the edge
　of History?"
 We invent gods
 to listen to our prayers
　to hold our hands
　 figuratively speaking
at those moments
 when we remember
　our fond mortality

If you hide y'r head in the sand
 you'll get it in your eyes
　and up y'r nose
 and in y'r lips
　and wherever else
　 you hold eternity

the gardens
 at the edge of the sea
my grandmother's house
 where we heard the news

two bombs
 and the war was over
but still the sun
 would not come out

113

War brings no joy
 even the end of war
brings no joy
 a long time
  before the nightmares
    cease

Imagination
full of the bones of history
and the dread
 broard arrows
  across the face of maps
and the words
 between the two of us
  the silent words
that lie like knives
 between the two of us

and the darkness
 is at hand
who wields the darkness?
 woven with so many dreams
  how can we sleep?

 a bus trip up country
along the rivers
 through the mountains
inland towns
 shopping malls
  and railroad tracks

How many times this journey?

The warm October sun
 the blue hemisphere of the sky
yellow green of the Prairie
 a nearly empty bus

running south now
 a line of mountains
in the distant west

an ancient image
across the carved up land

Dennis the Menace strikes again
 on the video
the childhood of a blond
 American kid
the instant TV reality
 more real than the mountains

 A bus going south
through a landscape of tears

 Collecting sticks to make a fire
building bridges in the air
weeding the garden
 fixing the roof

trying again to touch reality

(*what makes the ceiling waterproof?*
Landor's tarpaulins on the roof—W.B.Yeats, yeah really)

All journeys are epic
 even a bus ride to Edmonton
  and back
   via Kamloops
    Tete Jaune Cache
    and Calgary

Rain down on the coast
 first snow
  as we came out of the mountains
in Edmonton
 the last of summer
and Calgary
 from muggy heat
  to the breath of winter

Leaves blown in little circles
 in the corners by the buildings
  the dry dry cold

(Well I got a book
gotta put words in it
sent me by Serena
gotta do her justice

(Fatherhood
  like a stained and torn raincoat
   like I wear around the city streets
  and I wonder
  when poems will come again
              Hi Rhetoric!)

The flute player in the streets
counting my money in Calgary Public Library
I think I've made enough
  to ride the streetcar/train
and walk across the bridge
  to Kensington
   to look for Sheri-D
who's not in the store today
Try to make a poem out of that
  count those limping feet—

It's getting cold
 I'm getting old
  I won't get rich this way

Victims of infinity
who knows who ever we might be
 inconscionable

 eyes
the flaming eyes of love
and language flows
 from our finger tips

 Well I'm sixty years middle-aged
these are my mediaeval years
and I know that things
  won't go on for ever
but I'm only afraid that things
  in general, world wide I mean

will collapse
before this pile of guts and bones
 and nipples and dingle dangles
  that I call a body
   does

I really don't want to be around
 to watch the apocalypse
  thank you all the same
though it might be a great game

for Virtual Reality will rise up
 and swallow us
All we have left
 is virtual reality

the final game
 that we embraced
  we have become

here we are
this is us
 a flikker on the screen

return us to the earth, please

 and the proof of the pudding
but who'd go out
 in the cold night
  to find the proof of the pudding?

And suddenly we are awake
to find history knock knocking
 at our door
history with his bag of lies
 like a chimney sweep

or the gentle scratching
 that the future makes
announcing herself like a cat
 wanting to come in from the cold

later
 the loud insistent rapping
of the fate
that we all
 keep hidden away
  deep in our being
 even as children
  our bodies knew its hiding place
   within us
how casually we play
 with that little shiny key
  the key to all our being
turn the key
 and we fall apart
arms legs trunk head
 and all the rest
 like a puzzle toy

 our educated silences
disembodied consciousness
 locked up inside a microchip

We've decided that we live
 through our sundry differences
It was once a verb we lived thru'
 I (verb) therefor I am
(a thinker thort that thort
 and said
  "I am a thinker ergo sum,
more than orl U blokes")
 now it's all nouns
Got such and such ergo sum
 but who really cares
  who ergo sum

I get up in the morning
 pull on my best blue jeans
  ergo sum
drink two cups of tea
 or coffee
  go off to work
  ergo sum

come home
 drink a beer
  turn on the TV ergo sum
I am cogniscant of the patterns
 on the screen
  ergo sum

but have we forgot
 to celebrate
  our amness?
(I love ergo sum)
they got me on their files
 ergo sum

but if this consciousness
 slips from the earth
  or only evermore resides
   in microcircuitry
for that is possible
 with the present state of nolege
human consciousness
 could be replaced
  with computer consciousness
     Klik klik beep beep
 and if a tree falls in the forest
and only a machine is there to observe
 who among the angels
  its crashing down
   would ever care to listen?

and if our machines watch
 observe
  spin equations
   make decisions
who will lament the human race
 our precious individuality
  the planet of impossibility

and you ask for a key
 we pride ourselves
  that we could bring it all to dust
   maybe

and in the garden then
 of our despair
  a broken web
   of silences
you laugh aloud so longingly
 we are afraid
  we always are afraid
the whole kit and kerbooble
 of the human race
  shakes with laughter
   and fear

 You write the book of our return
 you can not imagine the future after us
 "History is at an end" so you believe
 "Nothing more can happen"
 "Time is an irrelevance"
 the world is just an expanded data base
  no more cold war
   that was so modernist
 they're all hot now
  we have entered the new chaos
 the post-mod dark age dawns
  an interesting sky!

 Anger Management
 international anger management
 but anger can only be managed so far
  till the genie bursts the bottle

We can no longer permit
 the chaos of history
but history does not wait
 upon permission

And all those wise guys
 who put a fix on it
at the edge of our discovery
 the future moves on
at a terrible pace
 and in the secret moments
of the continental drift

we spin continually
the live wire of our fear

and the children of history
 and the torturers
the old men in the citadels
 and the young soldiers
who are taught the ancient arts
 of obtaining information
 from unwilling subjects
all in the name of honour
 love of a country
the polished badges of their uniform
 and the unlaid ghosts
  of ancient battle fields

and where are we now
 and where are we going
riding the ferry to town again
 and the foghorn sounds
  through the cafeteria

 The leaves red and gold
across the soccer field
 from SUB cafeteria
where I sit here drinking tea

 dry october day
cold winter promised
 lots of snow, they say

and now again I'll go out
 and play the flute
to the 'Goddess of Democracy'

 and words
with such a terrible burden
 of meaning

the history of our human race
 and all the other species
 and systems

it's come in contact with
these last few centuries

We created God
 (the theological engineer
 is all of us, when drunk)
to encompass all the mystery
 of the universe
and the biological
 pleasure garden

Can we give our god
 an infinite capacity
  for forgiveness
to smile just a little
 once again
on the poor dumbfounded
 and benighted
  human race?

Our language points
 its accusing finger at us
  or do we blame
  Old Ma Gaia
who evolved us
 the most perfectly selfish creature
  short-sighted to a fault
yet diabolically clever
 in little things

an omnivore
 eat everything
  and then come back for more

 eat your way
to hell
 in a handbasket
here we go again
 consume consume

Could it have been different
 all things considered?

Were we doomed from the very beginning
 by the evolution of our upstart
cleverness?

 We only bit the apple
we didn't plant the bloody tree!
 and if the viruses don't do their job
  there won't be nothing left

and all of language
 hung out like a skin
  in the drying wind

 and back on E Broardway
the song they played on the radio
in Pancake Jacks that day
 such a long way from anywhere

Knowledge of the word
 ant's armies
  and cockroach nests
the friendly scorpion
 the eyes of time

an old man sits by the side of the road
 waiting for a bus
teenagers flicking spitballs
 at passers-by
  and laughing
and the long legged ladies
 of the night
  in their shiney thigh boots
and proud defiant strut
 'are you man enough for me?'
but do you know the way home
 any more?
you have only these undisputable
  questions
 Do we even deserve an answer?

    1995

COMPOST

The Poit
 in this untidy world
and as you say
 the poit in this untidy world
  drinks his tea

U say
 U gotta make a poim
  outa this
everything must be made
 into poims
 crafted into poims
  beaten into poims
melted down and molded
 into poims
 composted
  mixed with dung
   and tilled into poims
 dug into poims
or inflated with hot breath
 and blown into poims

Sitting in a downtown café
 in Nanaimo of a wet evening
in early Detzember
 wondering
  if this can't be made into a poim
then wot the hell can?

Such is life
 and wot is life
  but sum kind of atempt
   to make a poim?

scribble scribble scribble

Published in *Trying to Ryt a Poim*, 2000.

Independent books for independent readers since 1985

Selected Titles

cauldron books series

1. *Shadowy Technicians: New Ottawa Poets*. ed. rob mclennan, ISBN-13 978-0-921411-71-0
2. *This Day Full of Promise*. Michael Dennis, ISBN-13 978-1-896647-48-7
3. *resume drowning*. Jon Paul Fiorentino, ISBN-13 978-1-896647-94-4
4. *Groundswell: the best of above/ground press, 1993-2003*. ed. rob mclennan, ISBN-13 978-1-55391-012-1
5. *Dancing Alone: Selected Poems*. William Hawkins, ISBN-13 978-1-55391-034-3
6. *ancient motel landscape*. shauna mccabe, ISBN-13 978-1-55391-041-1

European Poetry Series

1. *Dark Seasons: A Selection of Georg Trakl poems*. ISBN-13 978-1-55391-049-7

Poets' Corner Award Series

1999. *Tales for an Urban Sky*. Alice Major, ISBN-13 978-1-896647-11-1
2001. *Starting from Promise*. Lorne Dufour, ISBN-13 978-1-55391-026-8
2002. *Peppermint Night*. Vanna Tessier, ISBN-13 978-1-896647-83-8
2003. *All the Perfect Disguises*. Lorri Neilsen Glenn, ISBN-13 978-1-55391-010-7
2004. *Republic of Parts*. Stephanie Maricevic, ISBN-13 978-1-55391-025-1
2006. *Heart's Cupboard*. Edward Gates. ISBN-13 978-1-55391-051-0

+

Antimatter. Hugh Hazelton, ISBN-13 978-1-896647-98-2
aubade. rob mclennan, ISBN-13 978-1-55391-039-8
Cuerpo amado / Beloved Body. Nela Rio, ISBN-13 978-1-896647-81-4
During Nights That Undress Other Nights / En las noches que desvisten otras noches. Nela Rio,
    ISBN-13 978-1-55391-008-4
Eyes of Water. Pauline Michel, ISBN-13 978-1-55391-044-2
Funambule / Tightrope, Pauline Michel, ISBN-13 978-1-55391-044-2
Garden of the Gods. Dina Desveaux, ISBN-13 978-1-55391-016-3
Herbarium of Souls. Vladimir Tasić, ISBN-13 978-0-921411-72-7
Impossible Landscapes, Tony Steele, ISBN-13 978-1-55391-037-4
Inappropriate Behaviour. Tim Lander, ISBN-13 978-1-55391-038-1
Jewelweed. Karen Davidson, ISBN-13 978-1-55391-048-0
Let Rest. Serge Patrice Thibodeau, ISBN-13 978-1-55391-035-0
The Longest Winter. Julie Doiron, Ian Roy, photos + fiction, ISBN-13 978-0-921411-95-6
Manitoba highway map. rob mclennan, ISBN-13 978-0-921411-89-5
notes on drowning. rob mclennan, ISBN-13 978-0-921411-75-8
Paper Hotel. rob mclennan, ISBN-13 978-1-55391-004-6
Poems for the Christmas Season. Robert Hawkes, ISBN-13 978-1-55391-033-6
Postcards from Ex-Lovers. Jo-Anne Elder, ISBN-13 978-1-55391-036-7
The Robbie Burns Revival & Other Stories. Cecilia Kennedy, ISBN-13 978-1-55391-024-4
Song of the Vulgar Starling. Eric Miller, ISBN-13 978-0-921411-93-2
The Space of Light / El espacio de la luz. Nela Rio; ed. E.G. Miller, short fiction & poetry,
    ISBN-13 978-1-55391-020-6
Speaking Through Jagged Rock. Connie Fife, ISBN-13 978-0-921411-99-4
Túnel de proa verde / Tunnel of the Green Prow. Nela Rio, ISBN-13 978-1-896647-10-4

www.brokenjaw.com hosts our current catalogue, submissions guidelines, manuscript award competitions, booktrade sales representation and distribution information. Directly from us, all individual orders must be prepaid. All Canadian orders must add 6% GST/ HST. CRA Number: 892667403RT0001.
Broken Jaw Press Inc., Box 596 Stn A, Fredericton NB E3B 5A6, Canada.